Quick

Computer Terms

Susan Davis Sherwin

Dictation Disc Company
14 East 38 Street, New York, NY 10016

INTRODUCTION

This book was written in self defense. What else could I do? I live with someone who can't figure out how to set the timer on the stove, but can take a computer apart and put it back together again better and faster than new.

And I have to deal this MIS guy who isn't very friendly and yells if you don't know whether your computer has a bozo bit or bit-mapped graphics.

The definitions I found in computer dictionaries were too complicated, too lengthy and not written for someone like me — a non-techie trapped in the computer age.

I hope you'll find it useful.

Author:

Susan Davis Sherwin

Technical Editors:

Steven Parrella

Alphonse Ferrara III

Editor:

Kathy Madden Berkemeyer

abort
To stop a program, a command or procedure before completion.

absolute address
A fixed location in the memory of the CPU, as opposed to a relative address, which is specified according to its distance from another location. Same as machine address, real address.

accelerator board
An adapter with a microprocessor that makes a computer run faster.

access
To retrieve; to use data or a file.

access time
The time it takes to retrieve data and make it available for the computer to process.

accumulator
The place in the CPU where the computer stores temporary information.

acoustic coupler
A modem that fits around a standard telephone handset to connect the computer to phone lines.

active
The program or part of a program currently in use.

Ada
A high level programming language developed by and for the military.

ADB (Apple Desktop Bus)
An interface in the Apple Macintosh computer used to connect input devices such as the keyboard and mouse.

add-in/add-on
Add-ins are the components (expansion boards, cartridges or chips) that can increase a computer's capabilities such as memory, graphics, communications. Add-ons usually refer to an entire circuit board.

add

address
A location within the memory of the computer.

aggregate function
A command that performs calculations based on a set of values rather than on a single value.

alert box
A small box that appears on screen with a cautionary warning. Same as message box.

algorithm
Clearly defined mathematical steps to solving a problem.

aliasing
The stair-step distortions in a computer-generated graphic image. Same as sawtooth distortions.

alphanumeric
All letters in the alphabet and numbers 0 through 9.

Alt (Alternate) key
A key, frequently used with other keys, to generate commands. Standard on all IBM PC and compatible computer keyboards.

ALU (Arithmetic Logic Unit)
The part of the computer's CPU that controls arithmetic computations.

AMD
A microprocessor used in the development of personal computers.

Amiga
A family of powerful personal computers with extra microprocessors for graphics and sound generation produced by Commodore Business Machines.

analog
A form of measurement with a continuous, infinite number of variations, i.e., a watch with hands, as opposed to digital counters, which go from one number to the next, with no in-between measurement.

analog computer
A type of computer, widely used in laboratories to measure on-going, continuous changes and record those changes on charts of graphs.

ana

analog/digital converter
Enables a digital computer to accept analog (usually laboratory measurement) input.

analog monitor
The type of color screen used in televisions.

ANSI (American National Standards Institute)
An organization of computer companies and others that promotes the development of standards for the computer industry.

ANSI.SYS
A device that makes a monitor on DOS and OS/2-based systems conform to ANSI standards.

antiliasing
The automatic smoothing out of stair-step distortions in a computer-generated graphic image.

API (Applications Program Interface)
Routines, protocols and tools for building software applications and user interface features, such as pull down menus and windows.

append
To add something at the end of a file or database.

Apple II
A family of personal computers featuring built-in sound and graphics produced by Apple Computer.

AppleTalk
A local area network standard developed by Apple Computer to link as many as 32 computers and peripherals.

AppleWorks
An integrated software package produced by Apple Computer for their Apple II computers.

application
The use of a computer for a specific purpose, i.e., designing a brochure, writing a letter, etc.

application software
Programs that perform specific tasks, such as word processing or database management.

architecture
The design of hardware and/or software.

archival backup
Backing up only files that have been changed since the last backup.

archive
Copying files for long term storage.

ARCnet
A type of local area network developed for office automation.

argument
Words, phrases or numbers entered on the same line as a command to expand or modify that command.

argument separator
A comma or other punctuation mark in a command or statement used to separate one argument from another.

arithemetic expression
An expression representing a numeric value.

ARLL
An encoding method used by hard disks and controllers.

ARPANET
A wide area network created by the US Defense Advanced Research Project Agency (ARPA) to link universities and research centers and support advanced scientific research.

Artificial Intelligence (AI)
The science of making computers play games, make decisions, understand human languages, even see and hear like humans.

ASCII (American Standard Code for Information Interchange)
A code representing English characters as numbers, which can be read by most computer software. Allows the transfer of data from one computer or word processing system to another.

ascender
The portion of a lowercase letter that rises above the height of the lowercase letter x.

assembler
A program that translates assembly language to machine language so that a computer can execute a program.

assembly language
Languages that tell the computer what to do in precise detail. Same as machine language.

assign
To give.

async
Short for asynchronous.

asynchronous
Not occurring at predetermined intervals, not synchronized.

asynchronous communication
Transmitting data intermittently rather than in a steady stream.

AT (Advanced Technology)
The IBM AT PC was introduced in 1984 with an Intel 80286 microprocessor, a 1.2MB floppy drive and an 84 key AT keyboard.

AT bus
The 16-bit expansion bus used in the IBM PC AT.

attenuation
The loss of signal strength in local area networks when the maximum range in that network's specifications is exceeded.

attribute
In word processing, a character emphasis, such as **boldface**, *italic*, underline. In databases, sometimes means field.

audit trail
In accounting programs, automatically keeping track of transactions.

AutoCAD
A computer-aided design program developed by AutoDesk.

AUTOEXEC.BAT
(AUTOmatic EXECute BATch file)

The main file that tells the computer what to do when it's turned on. It literally automatically executes a *batch* of files. This is where you would insert commands that you always want the computer to execute, such as display the date and time.

autotrace

A command that transforms a bit-mapped image into a vector image. Used in illustration programs.

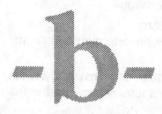

backbone

A wire that connects nodes, just like a bus.

background

In a computer that's handling more than one task at a time, background refers to the process that cannot accept input from the keyboard or mouse, but can access data stored on a disk. Also, the area of the screen not covered with characters and graphics.

backlighting

Used to make flat-panel displays easier to read.

backslash

\ Used to separate directory names and filenames in a DOS system.

backspace

A key that moves the cursor back one space, usually deleting the character that was in that space.

backup

Another copy of a file.

BACKUP

In DOS and OS/2 systems, an external command to make a copy of a file while preserving the original.

backward compatible
Compatible with earlier versions of a product.

backward search
Searching from the cursor's current position to the beginning of a document.

bad sector
A part of a floppy or hard disk that doesn't work.

bandwidth
Transmission capacity. In digital communications channels, usually measured in bits or bytes per second. In analog devices, it's measured in cycles per second or Hertz.

base address
A location that serves as a reference point.

base font
The font a word processing program automatically selects, unless instructed otherwise.

base memory
The portion of a computer's memory map used for user programs.

BASIC (Beginner's All-purpose Symbolic Instruction Code)
Simple programming language.

batch file
A series (batch) of DOS commands.

batch processing
When the computer executes a series of program instructions one after the other without user intervention. The opposite of transaction processing.

BAT file
Short for batch file.

baud rate
Transmission speed.

bay
Short for drive bay.

benchmark
Standard measure used to test performance.

benchmark program
Program used to test a computer's processing speed.

Bernoulli disk drive
Also called Bernoulli box. A special floppy disk drive that is faster and has greater storage capacity than traditional floppy drives.

beta site
Where a computer program is tested.

beta test
Testing computer software before commercial release.

Bezier curves
Mathematically defined curved lines.

binary
A number system consisting of just the digits 0 and 1.

binary file
A file stored in a binary format. Special software is required to display such a file.

binary search
A search that starts in the middle of a database, first determining if the desired record is above or below the mid point, then proceeding to the middle of the remaining records and so on.

BIOS (Basic Input/Output System)
Permanent software that's built into your PC. Controls functions including the boot up, keyboard, display screen, disk drives and other active systems in the computer. Usually encoded on a ROM (see Read Only Memory) chip and often referred to as ROM BIOS. Unaffected by disk failures, BIOS data can only be changed by changing the ROM chip.

bit (BInary digiT)
The smallest unit of information in a binary numbering system.

bit map
A graphics image consisting of rows and columns of dots.

bit-mapped font
A font with characters formed by a pattern of dots.

bit-mapped graphics
The technology used in TVs and most computer monitors where pictures are formed by a pattern of dots. Same as raster graphics.

BITNET
One of the largest wide area networks. Links colleges and universities in the US, Canada and Europe.

bits per second
See BPS.

blank character
The space produced by pressing the spacebar.

blank cell
In a spreadsheet or database, a cell that contains no values, labels or formatting.

blessed folder
A Macintosh System Folder, just like a DOS subdirectory, that contains files loaded at the beginning of an operating session.

block
In word processing, a selected section of characters. In data management, a group of records. In communications, a fixed batch of data that is transferred together.

block protection
Preventing a soft page break in the middle of a block of text.

BMP (Bit MaPped)
A standard file format that stores object-oriented graphics in device-independent form, enabling them to work in different systems and programs.

boilerplate
In word processing, selected words or phrases used over and over again.

bomb
To fail; to crash.

Boolean logic
A form of algebra in which all values are reduced to either true or false.

boo

Boolean operator

The symbol or word used to specify the inclusion or exclusion of criteria such as AND, OR, NOT, etc. Same as logical operator.

boot

The automatic routine that clears the memory, loads the operating system and prepares the computer for use. A cold boot is when the power is first switched on. A warm boot refers to restarting a computer that's already turned on (clearing the memory and reloading the operating system) without first switching it off.

box

An enclosed area on a screen. Like a window, but usually cannot be moved or resized.

bozo bit

Simple copy protection on a Macintosh system.

BPS (Bits Per Second)

Standard measure of data transmission speed.

break

A signal to stop processing or communications.

breakout box

A device used to separately test each electrical line in a communications cable.

bridge

A device that enables two networks to exchange data.

broadband

Data transmission where a single wire can carry several channels at once.

broadcast

Sending a message to more than one receiver.

browse

View data.

bubble jet printer

High quality print technology, equal in quality to ink jet printing.

buffer

An area that stores information temporarily, usually in RAM.

bug
A defect in hardware or software that causes a program to malfunction.

built-in font
Same as resident font.

bulk storage
Mass storage.

bulletin board system (BBS)
An electronic message center.

bundled software
Software that comes with a computer.

burn-in
A test of computer components, which runs the system for a day or two to detect defective chips.

bus
A combination of wires and circuits that transport signals from one part of the PC to another.

bus mouse
A mouse connected to the computer with an adapter or expansion board.

bus network
A decentralized local area network with a single connecting line design. *See **ring network***.

button
A small outlined area in a dialog box that can be clicked with a mouse to select a command.

byte
The storage unit for a single character, usually equal to 8 bits.

C

A flexible, fast, high-level programming language used for a variety of applications from business programs to engineering.

cache memory

A special, extra fast part of RAM where frequently accessed information is stored. Same as memory cache and RAM cache.

CAD (Computer Aided Design)

Hardware and software used by engineers and architects to design everything from houses to airplanes.

CAD/CAM (Computer Aided Design/ Computer Aided Manufacturing)

CADD (Computer Aided Design and Drafting)

CAE (Computer Aided Engineering)

CAI (Computer Aided Instruction)

calculated field

A data field that contains the results of calculations.

call

A programming instruction to transfer control to a subroutine, procedure or function.

callout

Text that identifies parts of an illustration.

capture

To save.

card

Electronic circuit board that fits into a computer's expansion bus slots.

carriage

Printer part that feeds paper.

cartridge

A removable storage part or module.

cascading windows
Over-lapping on-screen windows.

case sensitivity
A program's ability to distinguish between upper and lower case letters.

CRT (Cathode Ray Tube)
The technology behind most computer and television screens.

CDI (Computer Disc-Interactive)
Home entertainment and information technology developed by Philips that combines video, audio and text and stores it on a compact disk, which an be played on a CDI video machine attached to a television monitor.

CD-ROM (Compact Disc-Read Only Memory)
A read-only optical disk capable of storing large amounts (up to 250,000 pages) of data.

cell
A box in a spreadsheet where data can be entered.

cell address
The code for the location of a cell.

cell animation
The process of moving celluloid sheets over a stationary background to simulate movement.

cell definition
The contents of a cell in a spreadsheet.

cell format
The way a spreadsheet program displays the contents of cells on screen.

Central Processing Unit
See CPU.

Centronics interface
The standard interface for connecting printers and other parallel devices.

CGA (Color Graphics Adapter)
A color graphics system for IBM PCs and compatibles. Provides less resolution than EGA or VGA monitors.

CGM (Computer Graphics Metafile)
A standard file format that stores object-oriented graphics in device-independent form, enabling them to work in different systems and programs.

chained printing
Printing separate files as a unit.

chamfer
A beveled edge between two intersecting lines.

channel
A communications path between two devices. Also, an expansion bus for IBM PS/2 computers.

channel access
The method of gaining access to the data communication channel that links computers in local area networks.

character
Any symbol that is produced on screen by pressing a key.

character based
Capable of displaying only ASCII characters (as opposed to windows).

character mode
See text mode.

character set
Keyboard strokes recognized by the computer's hardware and software.

character string
A series of characters, usually set off by quotation marks, that are treated as a group. Same as string.

chassis
The metal frame/structural support that houses the computer's circuit boards and wiring.

checksum
A simple error-checking technique used in data communications.

chip
A miniaturized electronic circuit embedded in a small (usually 1/4 inch square or less) wafer of semiconducting material (usually silicon). Same as silicon chip.

Chooser
A desktop accessory that governs the selection of printer drivers in Macintosh computers.

circuit board
A thin piece of plastic on which electronic components have been laminated.

CISC (Complex Instruction Set Computer)
A CPU that recognizes as many as 200 instructions.

clear
Erase.

click
To quickly press and release the mouse button.

client
A workstation connected to a local area network on which users run applications.

client based application
An application that can be used only by certain workstations in a local area network.

client server network
Distributing the resources in a local area network among all the personal computers in that network.

clip art
A collection of illustrations that can be inserted into documents.

clipboard
A temporary storage place where text or graphics are stored.

clock
Evenly spaced pulses generated by an electronic circuit to synchronize the flow of information through the computer as well as keep time.

clock speed
How fast a microprocessor executes instructions.

clone
A copy that performs the same as the hardware, software or computer on which it was based.

close
Finish and save.

closed bus system
When the computer's internal data bus does not contain receptacles and is not easily upgradable.

CLS
An internal command in DOS and OS/2 systems that clears the screen and places the cursor in the upper left hand corner.

cluster
A unit of storage that includes one or more sectors of a floppy or hard disk.

CMOS (Complementary Metal Oxide Semiconductor)
A semiconductor chip that uses less power and is widely used in portable computers. Also used to keep basic set-up information, i.e., size of drive, type of monitor, etc. in a standard CPU.

coaxial cable
A high bandwidth connecting cable. More expensive than ordinary telephone wire, but can carry more data.

COBOL (Common Business Oriented Language)
A high level programming language specially designed for business applications that run on large computers.

code
Symbols representing something else. Most computer programs are written in code.

cold boot
Starting a computer by turning on the power.

collision
A jumbled transmission caused when two or more workstations on the same local network cable transmit at the same time.

color graphics adapter
See CGA.

column
A vertical line of characters or block of cells.

COM file
An executable program file with a .COM filename extension that operates in a specific part of the base memory in DOS and OS/2 systems.

COMDEX (Communications and Data Processing Exposition)
Computer trade show.

command
Instruction.

COMMAND.COM
A disk file that contains the command processor, and must be present on the start-up disk for DOS to run.

command processor
The part of the operating system that receives and executes operating commands and displays messages.

communications program
Software that gives a computer the ability to communicate with other computers over telephone lines.

communications protocol
A set of rules that govern the communications between computers over telephone lines. Both computers must have the same settings and follow the same standards for communication to be successful. Same as protocol.

comp
Short for "comprehensive" layout showing what a printed page will look like.

COMP command
In DOS and OS/2, a command that compares two or more text files to see if they're identical.

compatible
Indicates that one program or device can work with another.

compact disk (CD)
A read-only plastic disk that uses optical storage techniques to store large amounts of music or digitally encoded computer data.

compile time error
An error that occurs while a program is being compiled, as opposed to run time errors that occur while a program is being run.

compiler
A program that transforms a programming language into a machine-readable executable program.

Complementary Metal Oxide Semiconductor
See CMOS.

composite video
A standard type of video where red, green and blue signals are mixed together.

compressed file
A file written onto a special disk that minimizes the storage space required.

CompuServe
A large, public on-line information service. One of the first fee-based services for PC users.

computer
A machine capable of responding to instructions in a defined manner and performing a prerecorded list of instructions.

computer aided design
See CAD.

computer aided manufacturing
See CAM.

computer assisted instruction
See CAI.

Computer Graphics Metafile
See CGM.

computer system
An entire computer installation, including peripherals such as disk drives, monitors and printers.

CON
Refers to the keyboard and monitor in DOS and OS/2. Also, another way to refer to a PC console.

concatenation
Combining two or more units of information so that they form a single unit.

concurrency management
Ensures that data files in local area networks are not corrupted by simultaneous modification or input.

condensed type
A typeface with narrower-than-normal characters.

CONFIG.SYS (CONFIGuration SYStem)
An ASCII text file for DOS and OS/2 systems that contains commands.

configuration file
A file that contains information on the way a system is set up.

connectivity
A computer's or program's ability to link with other programs and devices.

connector
The part of a cable that plugs into a port to connect one device to another.

console
A monitor and keyboard.

constant
A value that never changes.

context sensitive help
The feature of a program that changes depending on what you are doing in the program, i.e. on-screen help programs.

context switching
The immediate activation of a program loaded into RAM.

contiguous
Next to, adjacent.

Control-break
In DOS and OS/2, a keyboard command that stops whatever program is running.

cont

control key
The key on IBM PC keyboards that is used in conjunction with other keys to perform tasks.

control panel
In Macintosh systems, a desk accessory that allows you to set many of the system parameters. In Lotus 1-2-3, the top three lines of the screen that contain program information. In OS/2 Presentation Manager, a utility menu that lists user options.

control program
See operating environment.

control unit
The part of the CPU that gets program instructions and carries them out.

controller card
An adapter that connects disk drives to the computer.

conventional memory
The portion of memory in a DOS system left available for running programs, over and above the memory used for system
use. Same as user memory.

convergence
The sharpness of a color graphics image.

coprocessor
The special processing unit that assists the CPU in performing certain operations. Same as math coprocessor, numeric coprocessor.

copy
Text. Also duplicate; the command used to duplicate a file.

copy protection
Techniques to prevent the unauthorized copying of software. Same as software protection.

corrupted file
A file with distorted data.

cpi (characters per inch)
The number of printed characters that fit into a linear inch.

CP/M (Control Program for Microprocessors)
One of the first PC operating systems, now nearly obsolete.

cps (characters per second)
A measurement of the speed of dot matrix and daisy wheel printers.

CPU (Central Processing Unit)
The main "box," or control section, which contains the hardware. The brain of the computer, where memory is stored, disks are inserted and most calculations take place. Same as microprocessor, system unit.

crash
Computer failure.

CRC (Cyclic Redundancy Check)
A technique for detecting data transmission errors.

crosstalk
Interference generated by cables too close to one another. Also, a communications program for IBM PCs and campatibles.

control-break
In DOS, keystrokes that cancel the previous command.

current cell
In a spreadsheet, the active cell.

current drive
Default drive.

cursor
A blinking character that indicates where the next keyboard stroke will appear.

customer support
Service to help customers with hardware and software problems and questions.

cut and paste
Move text from one place and insert it in another.

cut sheet feeder
See *sheet feeder*.

daisy wheel printer
A printer that produces letter quality type when characters, mounted in a circle, strike an inked ribbon.

DAT (Digital Audio Tape)
A data storage medium.

data
Information used to generate calculations or make decisions.

database
A computerized filing system, with easily retrievable information.

database management system (DBMS)
A group of programs that allow users to store, alter and retrieve information from a database.

data communications
The transfer of data, computer to computer.

data compression
Storing data in a format that requires less than usual storage space.

data dictionary
An on-screen listing of all of a database's files.

data entry
Entering data into a database.

data field
The space in a database for a specific piece of information.

data interchange format (DIF) file
A standard file format that allows the exchange of information among different spreadsheet programs.

data processing
Organizing and manipulating large amounts of computerized data.

data structure
How related pieces of information are organized.

dBase
A database management program for PCs.

debug
Find and correct programming errors.

dedicated
Reserved for one specific use.

default
A setting or value that's automatically chosen by the computer unless something else is specified.

defragmentation
A procedure that rewrites the files on a hard disk to speed up retrieval.

delimiter
A punctuation character, such as backslash or comma, that separates one section of a command from another.

demon
A program that waits until an event occurs before running; widely used to circumvent copy-protection procedures.

density
The amount of information that can be stored on a tape or disk.

descender
The portion of a lowercase letter that falls below the baseline.

desk accessory (DA)
A set of utility programs that are always available no matter what other applications are running.

desktop
On-screen graphics representation of computerized file systems.

desktop publishing
Producing high quality printed documents combining text and graphics on a PC.

DESQview
A program for IBM PC and compatibles that runs programs in a windowed, multitasking environment.

destination
Target.

device
Any piece of equipment that attaches to a computer.

device dependent
Programs that can only be run on a certain type of hardware.

device drivers
Software used to interface the operating system with existing installed hardware.

diacritical marks
Marks that indicate the phonetic value of a letter in a foreign language.

diagnostic
Test.

dialog box
An on-screen box that conveys or requests information from the user.

digital
When separate objects (digits) are used to stand for something so that counting and other operations can be performed precisely, going from one number to the next, with no in-between measurement.

digital monitor
A CRT (cathode-ray-tube) monitor that accepts digital signals and converts them to analog output.

digitize
Translate into digital form.

digitizer
A device that translates input into digital form, enabling you, for example, to enter sketches into a computer.

dingbat
A small star, bullet, flower, or other ornamental drawing used to enhance the appearance a document.

DIP (Dual In-line Package) switch
A group of small switches in a circuit board used to choose operating parameters.

direct-connect modem
A modem that connects directly to a phone line via modular connectors, rather than going through a telephone headset.

directory
A listing of files stored on a disk.

disk
See floppy disk, hard disk.

disk cache
A part of RAM used by the operating system to speed up access to frequently used data on a disk.

disk drive
A machine that reads data from and writes data onto a disk.

disk optimizer
Defragments a disk to speed up retrieval.

DISKCOMP
A DOS and OS/2 command that compares 2 disks to see if the information they contain is identical.

DISKCOPY
A DOS and OS/2 command that copies the entire contents (not just documents) of one disk (including hidden files) to another.

display screen
Monitor.

distributed database
A database with 2 or more files located at different network sites.

distributed processing
A computer system for multiple users that uses multiple computers.

dithering
When new colors and shades are created by varying the pattern of dots in a graphic.

divide overflow
Internal software error that occurs when an a program tries to perform a function that it cannot do.

DMA (Direct Memory Access)
A technique for transferring data from the main memory without passing through the CPU. Makes fast file copies.

documentation
Tutorials and reference material instructing how to use a computer system or program.

DOS (Disk Operating System)
The standard operating system for IBM-compatible personal computers. Same as MS-DOS.

DOS prompt
The letter informing DOS system users what drive they're in, followed by the greater-than symbol (C>), which indicates the system is ready to receive a command.

dot-matrix printer
Produces characters and graphics by striking pins against an ink ribbon.

dot pitch
An indication of the pixel size on a display screen. The lower the dot pitch number, the crisper the image.

double click
To click twice on a mouse button.

double density
When a disk can store twice as much data as a single density disk.

double sided
When a floppy disk can store information on both sides, holding twice the information of a single sided disk.

down
Off; not working.

downloadable font
Fonts which must be transferred from your computer to your printer in order to print.

downloading
Copying data from a main source to a peripheral device, i.e., loading a font into a laser printer.

downward compatibility
Software that can run on older and/or less powerful versions of the computer it was designed to run on.

DP
See data processing.

dpi (Dots Per Inch)
A measurement of the resolution of images.

draft mode
A faster, less than letter quality printer setting.

drag
Selecting and moving an on-screen icon via a mouse.

DRAM
See dynamic RAM.

drive bay
A reserved space in a computer where extra drives may be installed.

driver
A file or program that controls a monitor, printer or other device.

drop cap
A large letter at the beginning a paragraph positioned so that the top of the character is even with the top of the first line, the remainder below.

drop out type
White characters on a black background.

dumb terminal
A keyboard and monitor, with no processing capabilities or disk drives of its own, that is networked with a CPU.

dump
Copying the contents of memory from one place to another. Same as memory dump.

duplex
See full duplex, half duplex.

duplex printing
Printing on both sides of the paper.

DVI (Digital Video Interactive)
Makes it possible for a computer to store and display moving video images.

Dvorak keyboard
An alternative keyboard designed for speed where, unlike the standard "QWERTY" keyboard, most words fall in the middle row of keys.

dynamic
When action is taken as needed, not in advance.

dynamic link
A method of connecting data shared by two programs so that, when data is updated in one, it is easily updated in the other with a simple command.

dynamic RAM (DRAM)
A RAM memory chip that stores memory as electrical charges and must be continually "refreshed" or it will lose its contents.

E-mail (Electronic mail)
Sending files or messages electronically to users at distant terminals.

ECHO
ECHO mode in DOS and OS/2 displays a message on-screen as commands are being carried out.

edge connector
The part of a circuit board that connects to or plugs into the computer.

edit
Make changes to a document.

EGA (Enhanced Graphics Adapter)

A color graphics system for IBM PCs and compatibles that supports 16 colors. Provides higher resolution than CGA, lower than VGA.

EIA (Electronic Industries Association)

The national trade association involved in setting standards and representing all segments of the electronics industry.

EISA (Extended Industry Standard Architecture)

A 32-bit expansion bus for IBM PCs and compatibles that is downwardly compatible with existing 16-bit peripherals such as disk drives and display adapters.

echoplex

When the receiving station in an asynchronous communication acknowledges the receipt of a message by echoing the message back to the transmitting station.

electroluminescent display (ELD)

A type of very thin "flat panel" display screen popular for laptop and portable computers.

electronic mail

See E-MAIL.

em dash

A dash equal in width to the width of the capital letter M.

embedded formatting commands

Commands that affect how a document is printed, but cannot be seen on-screen.

EMM (Expanded Memory Manager)

The software program that manages EMS memory.
EMS (Expanded Memory Specification)
A technique of managing memory.

emulate

The ability of one device or program to duplicate the functions of another.

encryption

Encoding data so that it cannot be read without a password.

end

End key

A key on IBM PC and compatible keyboards that usually moves the cursor to the end of the line or the bottom of the screen, but can have different functions depending on which program is running.

end user

The ultimate user of a computer program or system.

endnote

A footnote at the end of a document.

Enhanced Expanded Memory Specification (EEMS)

Enables DOS applications to use more than 1MB of memory.

enhanced keyboard

A 102 key keyboard for IBM PCs and compatibles with function keys across the top.

enter/return key

The key that sends a command to the CPU.

entry line

In a spreadsheet, the line that displays the words you type.

environment

The basic hardware, software and program characteristics of your computer.

EOF (End Of File)

EOL (End Of Line)

erasable optical disk

A disk that can be erased and written on over and over again.

erasable programmable read-only memory (EPROM)

A type of memory chip that can be programmed, erased, and programmed again by manufacturers using ultraviolet light and a special programmer.

erase

Delete.

ergonomics

The science of designing safe, body conforming, comfortable machines, furniture — anything at all — that people use.

error detection

Techniques for detecting errors in a program or disk.

error trapping

The ability to recognize an error and respond appropriately.

Escape key

A key used to cancel the previous command.

ESDI (Enhanced Small Device Interface)

An enhanced interface for connecting hard disk drives and allowing faster access times.

Ethernet

A local area network hardware standard.

Excel

A powerful spreadsheet program for Macintosh and IBM PCs and compatibles.

executable file

A file in "computer language" that can be instantly executed by the computer.

execute

To run, to perform an action.

EXE file

An executable file with an .EXE extension in a DOS based system. Similar to COM files, but usually larger (not limited to 64K) and take longer to load. Most large programs are stored as EXE files.

expanded memory

A technique for utilizing more than 1MB of main memory, the amount of memory built into DOS-based computers. Conforms to EMS (Expanded Memory Specification) standards.

expansion board

An electronic card that inserts into a computer, giving it added capabilities such as increasing the amount of main memory.

expansion bus
A collection of wires in the computer that allow for the insertion of an expansion board.

expansion slot
Where the expansion board is inserted in the computer. Same as slot.

expert system
A program with extensive information on a particular subject.

export
To file data in a format that can be read by another program.

expression
In programming, refers to any set of symbols that represent a value.

extended memory
Memory added above and beyond the standard (1MB) of memory built into DOS computers. Unlike expanded memory, extended memory is not configured any special way.

extension
Letter or letters after the period in a DOS file that describe the file contents.

external command
In DOS and OS/2 systems, a command that will only work if the program file is in the current drive or directory.

external hard disk
A hard disk separate from the computer, designed to plug into an external port.

external modem
A modem separate from the computer, designed to plug into the computer's serial port.

fatal error
An error that causes a program to abort.

fault tolerance
The ability of a computer system to handle internal hardware problems without interrupting the system's performance.

fax
Short for facsimile. To send or receive a printed page over telephone lines.

fax modem
Attaches to a personal computer, giving it the ability to send or receive electronic messages over telephone lines.

feathering
Adding space between lines to center a page top to bottom.

field
The space designated to enter information.

file
An assortment of information stored as a single unit.

file allocation table (FAT)
A table used by the operating system to locate files on a disk.

file server
A computer the allows users in a local area network to share data and program files. Same as network server.

filespec
In DOS systems, a file's drive letter, pathname, filename and extension.

file transfer protocol
Governs the error-free transmission of asynchronous communications over telephone lines.

file transfer utility
A utility program that transfers files between different hardware, i.e, between a Macintosh and an IBM PC.

Finder
Along with System, makes up the desktop and file management system for Macintosh computers.

firmware
Permanent programs or data on read only memory.

fill
Entering a series of numbers, dates, times or formulas in a worksheet.

filter command
A DOS and OS/2 command that takes input from one source, changes or reduces it, and sends the result to another device or printer.

flag
Signal.

flat file database
A simple database management program that takes or stores information from only one file at a time.

flatbed scanner
An optical scanner with a flat surface that can copy a page into an electronic file.

flat panel display
A very thin display screen popular in laptop computers.

floating decimal point
Storing and calculating numbers so that the decimal moves as needed.

floppy disk
A magnetically sensitive, portable disk used for storing electronic data.

flush left/right
Aligning text along the left/right margins.

flow
A page layout where copy wraps around graphics.

folder
A storage place for multiple documents in Macintosh and other graphic user environments.

font
A complete set of letters, numbers and symbols with a common design.

font card
An expansion board that allows certain printers to print additional fonts.

font cartridge
A read only memory cartridge that allows certain printers to print additional fonts.

footer
Explanatory line or lines of copy that appear at the bottom of a printed page.

footnote
A note that appears at the bottom of a printed page.

footprint
The amount of space taken up by a computer or other device.

forced page break
A page break designated by the user.

foreground
The program currently on screen, activated and accepting keyboard commands.

format
To prepare a disk for reading, writing and accepting files.

form feed (FF)
Causing the printer to advance one page length at a time.

form software
A program that enables you to design and fill in forms on your computer

FORTRAN (FORmula TRANslator)
High level programming language.

fourth generation language (4GL)
A closer-to-human than usual programming language.

fragmentation
When files become scattered on a disk. Caused by frequent additions and deletions.

freeware
Programs that are not copyrighted and are free for public use. Same as public domain software.

friction feed
A dot matrix or daisy wheel printer paper feed method where paper is fed through a roller.

front end
Computers and programs that allow user-friendly access to other computers and databases.

full duplex
When data can be transmitted in two directions at once.

function
Specific task.

function keys
Keyboard keys that perform different functions depending on the program being used.

gas plasma display
See plasma display.

gateway
Hardware and software that connect two types of networks.

general format
The default numeric format in a spreadsheet which displays values with all significant decimal points, but no commas or currency signs.

gem

GEM
A graphical user interface built into some computers that provides a windowed environment for running programs.

GEnie
An on-line information service.

ghosting
The permanent etching of a pattern on a display screen, which can occur when a pattern is displayed undisturbed for long periods of time.

giga (G)
Represents one billion.

gigabyte
Represents one billion bytes.

global backup
Copying everything on the hard disk onto a floppy.

global format
The numeric format choice that applies to all cells in a spreadsheet program worksheet.

glossary
Frequently used phrases stored in a word processing program storage utility that can be inserted into documents as needed.

gppm (Graphics Pages Per Minute)
How fast a laser printer can print pages with graphics.

grabber hand
An on-screen image of a hand that's controlled with a mouse.

graphical user interface (GUI)
(pronounced gooey)
A device that makes a program more user friendly by using icons and windows instead of programming commands.

graphics
Pictures, sketches, graphs and other non-typed images.

graphics-based
Software and hardware that treat on-screen objects as bit maps or geometric shapes rather than characters.

graphics file format
How information to display graphics is stored on a disk.

graphics mode
When on-screen images are treated as pixels rather than characters.

graphics scanner
A device that transforms pictures into on-screen images.

gray scale
All the shades of gray, from white to black, used to represent an image.

greeking
Nonsense words and phrases used to represent the positioning of text in a layout.

groupware
Programs used by groups in local area networks.

guide
An on-screen, non-printing dotted line used to show the location of page breaks, margins, etc.

gutter
The space between columns in a multiple-column page layout.

GW-BASIC
A programming language.

hacker
Slang for a technically sophisticated computer enthusiast.

half duplex
When data can be transmitted in only one direction at a time. Same as local echo.

half height drive
A disk drive that uses half the usual space allotted to disk drives on IBM PCs and compatibles.

halftone
A pattern of black dots used to represent all the gradations of tones in a graphics image, like in newspapers.

handle
In graphics programs, the small black squares that surround an object to manipulate the object via a mouse.

handshaking
When one device signals to another that it's ready to transmit or receive a data communication.

hanging indent/hanging paragraph
When the first line in a paragraph is flush left, and the rest of the paragraph is indented.

hard copy
Printed-on-paper version of on-screen text or graphics. Same as printout.

hard disk
A non-floppy magnetic disk that stores computer data.

hard disk drive
The device that reads and writes data on a hard disk. Same as Winchester drive.

hard return
In word processing, a user-generated moving of the cursor to the beginning of the next line.

hard-wired
Functions built into the computer's electronic circuits.

hardware
Electronic components, boards, disks, display screens... any part of a computer system that can actually be touched.

hardware platform
See platform.

hardware reset
Soft reboot.

Hayes compatible
When a modem recognizes the commands of a Hayes-manufactured modem.

head
The device that reads data from and writes data to a computer disk or tape.

head crash
When a hard disk's head scratches or burns a disk. A serious problem.

header
A line or lines of copy that appear at the top of every page in a document.

help
On-screen instructions and advice.

Hercules
A monochrome monitor adapter capable of displaying graphics.

hertz (Hz)
The cycle-per-second measurement of electrical vibrations.

heterogeneous network
A network consisting of computers and devices from several manufacturers.

hexadecimal
A numbering system that consists of 16 unique symbols; the numbers 0 to 9 and the letters A to F.

hidden codes
Formatting codes embedded into a document, but invisible on screen.

hidden file
In DOS, a file with a "hidden attribute" doesn't appear on the disk directory, cannot be displayed, erased or copied, but can be viewed with most file management utilities.

Hierarchical File System (HFS)
Pyramid-like file system where each object is linked to those beneath it. Typical format for computer files with directories and subdirectories.

high density disk
Floppy disk capable of storing more information than double density disks.

high density disk drive
Capable of reading and formatting both high density and double density disks.

high end
High priced.

high level format
Creates sections on a disk to store specific information including the boot record and file allocation table. Same as logical format.

high level language
A programming language that resembles human speech and runs on different types of computers.

high memory (Himem.SYS)
The device driver that manages the first 64K above 1MB of DOS memory.

highlight
On-screen copy displayed in reverse or other notice-ably different type style.

hinting
Digitally reducing the weight of a small typeface so it will print clearly.

home computer
A personal computer designed for home use, usually with less capabilities and/or memory than a business PC.

home key
A key on IBM PC keyboards that has various functions depending on the program, but usually brings the cursor to the beginning or end of a page or document.

host
The computer in a network that contains data that can be accessed by other computers in the network.

hot key
A keystroke selected by the user to call up a memory resident program (a program that will run at all times, even within other applications) such as calendar or calculator.

hot

hot link
When applications are connected so that changes in one program (such as a database) are automatically made in another (such as a spreadsheet).

HP (Hewlett-Packard)
A company that produces printers, PCs and calculators.

HyperCard
A programming language for Macintosh computers.

hypertext
A type of database system than links objects so that related objects can be quickly and easily accessed. For example, highlighting the word "dogs" in an encyclopedia program might open a window to "small, medium, large" which could open a window listing different breeds, etc.

hyphenation
The splitting of a word so that it does not extend into the right hand margin.

I-beam pointer
A pointer used in many desktop publishing and word processing programs.

IBM PC
A family of personal computers produced by IBM and first introduced in 1981.

IBM PC AT (Advanced Technology)
An advanced model of the IBM PC XT introduced in 1984.

IBM PC XT (eXtended Technology)
An enhanced version of the IBM PC introduced in 1983.

IBM PC compatible

A computer by any number of manufacturers that runs software and can use hardware developed for IBM PCs.

IBM Personal System/2

Second generation IBM PCs introduced in 1987.

icon

A small on-screen symbol that represents an object, program or function.

IDE (Intelligent Drive Electronics)

A new generation of hard drives to compete with SCSI and ESDI interfaces.

identifier

Name.

if/then/else

A control that tests if a condition is true; then if it is true, goes on to one option, if false, goes on to another option.

illegal character

A character than cannot be used in certain command-driven programs because it is reserved for other functions, e.g. a DOS file name cannot contain an asterisk or comma because they serve other functions.

imagesetter

A professional typesetting machine.

impact printer

Printers that put images on paper when a head or character representation strikes a ribbon.

import

To copy data created by one program onto another.

incremental backup

When a backup is made only if and when files are modified, not at predetermined intervals.

indentation

Aligning a line or paragraph to margins inside those affecting the entire document.

ind

Industry Standard Architecture (ISA) bus
The bus used in IBM PC/XTs and PC/ATs (called the AT bus).

infection
Computer virus.

INIT
A utility program for Macintosh computers that executes during a system start or restart.

initialize
To format a Macintosh disk, to activate a computer printer and to format a PC disk.

ink jet printer
Produces high quality text and graphics by spraying ink at paper.

input
Information entered into a computer.

input device
Any mechanism that feeds information into a computer, such as a keyboard, mouse or modem.

input/output (I/O) system
Any operation, program or device that feeds information into or extracts data from a computer's CPU, such as a keyboard.

Ins (Insert) key
On IBM PC and compatible keyboards, the key that toggles between insert and overtype modes in most word processing programs.

insert mode
When a typed character pushes existing text to the right.

insertion point
The point where the next typed character will appear on screen.

installation program
A program that assists users in installing application software.

instruction
Computer command.

44

instruction cycle
The time the CPU takes to execute a command.

instruction set
Key words that describe all the capabilities of a CPU.

integer
A whole number.

integrated
When 2 or more components work together as a single entity.

integrated circuit (IC)
A chip or semiconductor circuit that contains more than one transistor and electronic component.

integrated program
A program than combines 2 or more software functions such as word processing and spreadsheets.

Integrated Services Digital Network
See ISDN.

intelligent terminal
A monitor and keyboard with processing capabilities.

Intel
The largest manufacturer of computer microprocessing chips, which make up the CPU.

interactive
Allowing user input.

interface
Connection.

interlacing
A display technique that increases monitor resolution.

interleaving
The configuration of sectors on a disk; also main memory.

internal command
In DOS and OS/2 systems, any command that remains in memory and resides in the COMMAND.COM file such as COPY and DIR.

internal font
A font built into the hardware of a printer.

internal modem

A modem on an expansion board that plugs into the expansion bus of a PC. Same as on-board modem.

interpreter

A program that translates and runs instructions written in a high-level programming language.

interprocess communication (IPC)

When one process of an operating system can communicate with another running on the same computer or network.

interrupt

An internal hardware command that temporarily stops one function so that another can take place.

invisible file

Hidden file.

I/O

See input/output system.

ISDN (Integrated Services Digital Network)

An international communications standard for sending data, voice and video over telephone lines.

italic

Fonts with characters slanted to the right.

iteration

See loop.

jaggies

The stair-step distortions in a computer-generated graphic image.

job

Task performed by your computer.

joystick

A handle-like mechanism that moves the cursor. Used mainly for computer games.

jump line

A notation at the end of a section of a story in any printed medium indicating where the story is continued.

jumper

A connector that closes an electrical circuit. Often used to customize circuit boards by changing a board's parameters.

justification/justify

Aligning lines of text along the right and/or left margins.

K

Short for kilobyte.

Kermit

A file transfer protocol used for more error-free modem communications.

kerning

Adjusting the space between characters, moving them closer to improve the look and readability of text; used in proportional type fonts.

key assignments

Functions that a computer program assigns to specific keys.

keyboard

Typewriter-like keys used to enter data into a computer. Consists of alphanumeric (letters, numbers), punctuation, control, arrow, delete, enter, escape, return, toggle and other special function keys.

keyboard template
A plastic or paper card placed on the keyboard to indicate a program's particular key designations.

keystroke
Pressing a key.

key word
A word with a special meaning that is recognized by the computer or program.

kilobit
1,024 bits of information.

kilobyte
1,024 bytes of information.

kludge
Slang for an improvised, not very good, solution to a problem.

label
Name.

label prefix
In a spreadsheet program, the punctuation mark preceding a cell entry.

LAN (Local Area Network)
Computers linked together in a relatively small area that share or exchange information.

landscape
In word processing, printing a page horizontally across the wider length of paper.

language
Communicating in such a way that an object (computer) or person understands what you are saying.

laptop
A small, portable, battery powered, lightweight computer.

large scale integration (LSI)
Placing thousands of electronic circuits on a single computer chip.

laser font
Clear, undistorted characters formed by a laser printer.

laser printer
Produces the highest quality print by fusing text and graphic images to the page.

latency
The delay in the actions of a disk drive caused by the rotation of the disk.

launch
Start.

layer
The ability of some programs to allow text or graphics to be placed in a number of independent "background" and "foreground" layers or "sheets."

layout
The position of text and graphics on a page.

LCD (Liquid Crystal Display)
A form of flat, low power display that uses rod-shaped crystal images to form letters and/or numbers.

leading
The measure of blank space between lines of text.

leading zeros
Zeros placed in front of a number to use up all blank spaces in a data field.

LED (Light Emitting Diode)
An electronic device that emits light when current flows through it.

letter quality (LQ)
The same quality of print produced by a high quality typewriter.

library
A collection of files or programs in the computer system.

library routines
A collection of routines or procedures used by a program to handle tasks.

LIFO (Last In, First Out)
See stack.

ligature
When two or more characters are designed so they're joined together for a more pleasing look, i.e., fi, ff, fl, ffi, ae and oe.

light emitting diode
See LED.

light bar
The highlighted section on a display screen indicating a menu selection.

light pen
A pen-shaped input device that uses a light sensitive detector to "write" on screen much the same way maneuvering a mouse does.

LIM (Lotus Intel Microsoft) memory
A technique for adding memory to a DOS system.

line
In programming, one program statement. In data communications, a circuit that connects two or more devices.

line adapter
An electronic device, such as a modem, that converts signals from one form (digital) to another (analog) so that they can be transmitted over telephone lines.

line art
A computer-drawn graphic without halftones that can be clearly printed.

line editor
A type of editor that allows only one line of a file to be edited at a time.

line feed (LF)
A signal to advance paper in the printer or the cursor on the screen to the next line.

line printer

A high speed printer than prints an entire line at once and is capable of printing as many as 3,000 lines a minute.

link

In spreadsheets, to establish a connection between two files so that a change in one is reflected in the other.

linker

A program that combines modules to form an executable program.

liquid crystal display

See LCD.

LISP (LISt Processor)

A high level programming language often used in artificial intelligence applications.

load

To install, or transfer instructions from a disk into RAM.

local area network

See LAN.

local area wireless network (LAWN)

A local area network that uses high frequency radio waves instead of wire connections between computers.

local echo

See half duplex.

LocalTalk

Connectors and cables manufactured by Apple for Macintosh computers and the AppleTalk network.

lock

Preventing users from updating or deleting a file.

logic board

See motherboard.

logical

Pertaining to software, as opposed to physical, which pertains to hardware.

log

logical format
See high level format.

logical operator
See Boolean operator.

Logo
A high level programming language.

log in/log on
To enter information into the computer so that it "recognizes" you as a valid user; allows a working session to begin. Used as a security measure in networks.

log off/log out
To end a working session on the computer.

loop
In programming, instructions that reappear continuously until a certain condition is met. Same as iteration.

Lotus 1-2-3
A flexible, easy to use spreadsheet program for IBM PCs and compatibles that combines graphics, spreadsheet functions and data management.

lower case
Small letters.

low level format
A formatting procedure generally done before a disk leaves the factory. Sometimes called a physical format. Prepares the disk for high level formatting, which establishes the housekeeping sections that track the free and in-use areas of the disk.

low level language
A machine or assembly programming language.

low resolution
Fuzzy image produced on a screen or by a printer.

LPT (Line Printer Terminal)
Identifies one of the parallel ports that can connect a parallel printer.

LQ
See letter quality.

LSI
See large scale integration.

M
Short for megabyte.

Mac
Short for Macintosh computer.

MacBinary
A file transfer protocol that allows Macintosh computer files to be stored in non-Macintosh computers without losing graphics, icons and other information.

machine address
Same as absolute address.

machine dependent
When a software application can run only on a particular type of computer.

machine independent
The ability of software to run on different types of computers.

machine language
Same as assembly language.

Macintosh computer (Mac)
A family of personal computers produced by Apple Computer featuring windows, icons and a mouse.

MacPaint
A paint program for Macintosh computers.

macro
A name or keystroke that represents a list of commands or actions for the computer to perform.

MacroMind Director
An animation program for Macintosh computers.

MacWrite
A Macintosh word processing program.

magnetic disk
See floppy disk, hard disk.

magnetic media
When magnetic materials are used to store and retrieve data on disks or tapes.

magnetic tape
A magnetically coated strip of plastic used to store data.

mail merge
Taking information from a database and inserting it in a word processing document. Often used to create "personalized" form letters from mailing lists.

mail box
Where electronic mail is stored until retrieved by the user the message is addressed to.

main memory
The computer's internal memory system.

mainframe
A large, expensive business computer with enough memory and power to support the needs hundreds of users.

main storage
See RAM.

male connector
A computer cable with pins protruding from the surface.

map
A list of the contents of a program.

mapping
Converting data from one format to another.

margins
The borders of blank space surrounding print or graphics on a sheet of paper.

mass storage
Bulk storage.

math coprocessor
Performs all necessary math computations so the CPU can concentrate on other tasks.

mathematical expression
An expression representing a numeric value.

maximize
In a windows program, enlarging a window to its largest size.

MB, Mbyte, Meg (MegaByte)
A measure equal to approximately one million bytes.

MCGA (Memory Controller Gate or Multicolor Graphics Array)
The graphics system built into many IBM PCs and compatibles.

media
Items on which data can be stored, including hard disks, floppy disks, tapes.

megaflop (MFLOP - Mega Floating-point Operations Per second)
A common measure of the speed of computers used to perform floating-point calculations. One MFLOP equals one million floating point operations per second.

megahertz (MHz)
A measure equal to approximately one million electrical vibrations per second.

membrane keyboard
A flat keyboard covered with a sheet of plastic picturing outlines of keys.

memory
A computer's primary, internal storage area. Same as RAM (Random Access Memory).

memory address
A code number for a specific location in the computer's RAM.

memory cache
See cache memory.

memory dump
See dump.

memory resident
Permanently in memory. Same as RAM resident.

menu
An on-screen list of choices of programs, functions or commands.

menu bar
A horizontal menu that appears on top of a window.

menu driven
A program that provides menus for choosing options.

merge
Combine.

message box
See alert box.

MFM
See modified frequency modulation.

microcomputer
Same as personal computer (PC).

micro disk, micro floppy
A 3 1/2" square floppy disk in a hard case.

microprocessor
An integrated circuit that contains a CPU.

Microsoft Corporation
A major computer software company.

Microsoft Excel
A powerful graphics-oriented spreadsheet program for IBM PCs and compatibles and Macintosh computers.

Microsoft Windows
An operating environment for IBM PCs and compatibles that features icons, pull down menus, desk accessories and the ability to easily move text and graphics from one program to another via a clipboard, and to operate more than one program at a time.

Microsoft Word
A popular, full-featured word processing program for a variety of computers.

Microsoft Works
A program that contains a word processor, spreadsheet, database, telecommunications utility and more for IBM PCs and compatibles and Macintosh computers.

microspacing
Justifying text by inserting variable sized spaces between letters.

MIDI (Musical Instrument Digital Interface)

A standard that enables computers and musical synthesizers and instruments to exchange information, allowing music to be composed, written and edited on computer keyboards.

migration

When computer users move from one hardware platform to another.

million instructions per second

See MIPS.

millisecond (ms)

One thousandth of a second.

minicomputer

In general, a computer more powerful than a PC, but smaller than a mainframe. Usually designed to allow anywhere from 4 or 5 to 100 to 200 users to work simultaneously.

MIPS (million instructions per second)

A measure of the rate that a computer executes microprocessor instructions.

MIS (management information system)

Software that provides managers of organizations with tools for evaluating their departments. Also describes Manager, Information Systems.

MKDIR (MD)

The internal DOS and OS/2 command to crate a subdirectory.

MNP (Microcom Networking Protocol)

A communications protocol used by many high speed modems.

mode

The operating state of a program, i.e., in word processing, by depressing a toggle switch, you could change from insert mode to typeover mode.

model

The representation of an object in pictures or numbers.

mod

modem (MOdulator-DEModulator)
A device that transmits data over telephone lines.

modified frequency modulation (MFM)
A method of recording digital information on tapes and disks.

modular architecture
A design consisting of self-contained components that can be connected together.

modulation
The conversion of a digital signal to analog.

Moire distortion
A flickering illusion that sometimes occurs when high contrast line patterns appear too close to one another.

monitor
Display screen. Same as video monitor.

monochrome
Single color.

monochrome display adapter (MDA)
A monochrome video adapter for IBM PCs and Pcompatibles that displays high resolution text, but not graphics.

monospace
When each character in a typeface is the same width.

motherboard
The circuit board that contains a computer's CPU, microprocessor support chips, RAM and expansion slots. Same as logic board, system board.

Motorola microprocessors
Used in Apple Macintosh and Commodore Amiga computers and many workstations.

mouse
A small input device on a rolling ball that controls the cursor's on-screen movements and contains one or more buttons that have different functions depending on the program.

mousepad
A pad used under a mouse to provide more traction for the mouse ball.

MS-DOS
(MicroSoft Disk Operating System)
Same as DOS.

Multicolor Graphics Array
See MCGA.

MultiFinder
A program for Apple Computers that enables the Macintosh to run more than one application at a time.

multifrequency monitor
A video monitor that can accept signals at more than one frequency range and support different video standards.

multifunction peripheral (MFP)
A device that combines the functions of several input/output devices.

multilaunching
When two or more users in a local area network open an application program.

multilevel sort
When the order in which data is displayed in a database program is determined by two or more data fields.

MultiMate
A word processing program.

multimedia
When audio, video, graphics and text are combined to present information.

multiplexing
Transmitting multiple messages simultaneously over one channel in a local area network.

multiscanning/multisync monitor
A color monitor that automatically adjusts to the frequency of the video display board it is connected to.

multitasking
The simultaneous running of two or more programs. Same as parallel processing.

multiuser
Computer systems that support two or more users simultaneously.

musical instrument digital interface
See MIDI.

name
Characters that identify a file or other entity.

nanosecond (ns)
One billionth of a second.

native file format
The format a program defaults to when storing data on a disk.

natural language
Human language, as opposed to computer programming language.

natural recalculation
In a spreadsheet program, when calculations are redone, incorporating data from all cells included in the calculation.

near letter quality (NLQ)
Not quite typewriter quality print from a dot matrix printer. Falls between letter quality and draft.

NetWare
A local area network operating system manufactured by Novell for IBM PCs and compatibles and Macintosh computers. It links hardware and accommodates many network interface cards, network architectures and several communications protocols.

network
Two or more computer systems linked together.

network administrator
The person responsible for maintaining local area networks and assisting users.

network architecture
The hardware, software and cable standards for a local area network.

network interface card (NIC)
An adapter that hooks a network cable directly to a microcomputer.

network operating system
Local area network software that runs on the file server and assists the flow of information among users.

network server
See file server.

network topology
The geometric arrangement of a local area network computer system. Same as typology.

network protocol
The rules and signals that networked computers use to communicate.

network version
An applications program revised to function in a network environment.

neural network
Type of computing that creates connections between processing elements, imitating the way the human brain works.

newspaper columns
Two or more vertical columns of text, with text flowing from the bottom of one column to the top of the other. Same as snaking columns.

NIC
See network interface card.

NiCad (NIckel CADmium) battery pack
Battery pack used for many portable computers.

NLQ
See near letter quality.

node
A computer or other device, such as a printer in a local area network, that can create, receive or repeat information.

noise
Random electrical signals on a communications
channel (caused by such things as electrical wires,
lightning, bad connections) that, when excessive, can
cause data loss.

nonimpact printer
A printer that causes an image without striking a head
against a ribbon. Includes inkjet and laser printers.

noninterlaced
When monitors do not use interlacing techniques to
improve resolution.

nonvolatile memory
Type of memory, such as ROM, that retains its
contents when power is turned off.

NOR operator
Boolean operator that gives a TRUE reading only
when both operands are FALSE.

Norton Utilities
Utility programs for IBM PCs and compatibles.

notebook computer
Lightweight (around 6 lbs) personal, portable
computer, considerably smaller than a laptop.

NOT operator
Boolean operator that gives a TRUE reading if its
operand is FALSE, and FALSE if the operand is TRUE.

ns
Short for nanosecond.

NTSC (National Television Standards Committee)
Sets the standards for the transmission of American
television. The NTSC standard is incompatible with
most foreign television standards and most computer
video signals.

NuBus
High speed Macintosh II expansion bus.

null character
A character with a numeric value of 0, frequently used
in programming languages to mark the end of a
character string.

null modem cable

A serial cable that connects two computers directly, without the need for a modem.

numeric coprocessor

See coprocessor.

numeric coprocessor socket

A socket on a motherboard into which a numeric coprocessor can be attached.

numeric keypad

Keys, usually located to the right of a keyboard, that display numbers 0 through 9 in a calculator-like configuration.

num lock key

A toggle key that locks the numeric keypad into the numbers mode, disabling those cursor movement keys.

object code

The computer programming machine-readable instructions produced by a compiler.

object oriented graphics

Images composed of lines, circles, boxes and other elements that can be independently moved. Not used in PC displays, but sometimes used for architectural or engineering design. Same as vector graphics.

object oriented programming

When programmers define the types of functions that can be applied to a data structure, as well as the data structure itself.

OCR

See optical character recognition.

oblique

The italic version of a sans-serif typeface.

odd

odd header
A header appearing only on odd-numbered pages.

odd parity
A type of error checking protocol for asynchronous communications using an odd number of set bits.

OEM (Original Equipment Manufacturer)
A company that manufactures hardware for other companies.

off-line
Not connected to a computer or communications network.

off-screen formatting
When formatting commands are embedded into the text, but are not visible on the screen.

offset
The blank space left along the edge of a printed sheet of paper.

on-board
On a circuit board.

on-board modem
See internal modem.

on-line
Connected to a computer.

on-line service
A service that can be accessed via modem. Popular ones give access to databases, bulletin boards, stock quotes, current events, shopping services, encyclopedias and much more.

OOP (Stands for Object Oriented Programming)

OOPL (Stands for Object Oriented Programming Language)

OOPS (Stands for Object Oriented Programming System)

open architecture
A computer system with public standards and specifications, which makes it easy to design add-on products, but also makes it easy to copy.

open bus system
An expansion bus that accepts various adapters.

operand
In computer language expressions, the objects that are manipulated.

operators
In computer language expressions, the symbols that represent specific actions, i.e., +, X, -, etc.

operating environment
The environment in which programs are run, i.e., DOS or windows. Same as control program.

operating system
The main program on a computer that manages the computer's internal functions and runs other programs.

optical character recognition (OCR)
The machine recognition/transfer of printed text into a form that the computer can manipulate.

optical disk
A storage medium, written and read by lasers, for large amounts of data. Currently, there are four types of optical disks: CD-ROM (with permanently encoded data that can be read any number of times), WORM (stands for Write Once, Read Many), and erasable (also called erasable optical or floptical disks), and CD-ROM XA (a Sony-developed technology that combines data, video, graphics and audio.)

optical scanner
A device that reads a page of text or graphics and translates it into a form the computer recognizes and can manipulate. Same as scanner.

ORACLE
A program that enables Macintosh and IBM PC and compatible users to access data from large corporate databases.

orphan
The first line of a paragraph that appears as the last line of a page.

OS/2 (Operating System/2)
An operating system invented by IBM that is designed
to run several programs at the same time and to take
the place of DOS for the most powerful IBM compatible personal computers. OS/2 can run all DOS
programs, but DOS cannot run all OS/2 programs.

outline font
A scalable font in which the outlines of the characters
are mathematically defined and then filled in by the
printer.

outline utility
A feature of some word processing programs that
assists users in organizing a document by creating an
outline.

output
The representation of computerized data.

output device
Any device, like a printer or display screen, that can
exhibit information from a computer.

overflow error
An error that occurs when the computer's predefined
range of values is exceeded.

overlaid windows
When windows on the screen are overlapped and
displayed one on top of another.

overstrike/overtype
The printing of a character directly on top of another.

66

pack
Compress data.

packaged file
A file in a compressed format.

packaged software
Software sold in stores, as opposed to customized programs.

pad character
Characters used to fill up empty spaces.

page break
The on screen indication of the end of a page. ·

page description language (PDL)
A programming language that describes the layout and contents of a page, such as Adobe PostScript and Hewlett Packard PCL (Printer Control Language).

page layout program
A program that allows users to precisely place graphics and text on a page, such as PageMaker and Ventura.

PageMaker
A page layout program for Macintosh and IBM PCs and compatible computers.

page mode memory
RAM that provides fast access by storing information in segments of rows and columns.

page orientation
The way type or graphics are printed on a page, horizontally or vertically, i.e., landscape or portrait.

page preview
See preview.

Page Up/Page Down keys
Moves the cursor to the beginning of the previous page, or the beginning of the next page.

pagination
Numbering pages.

paint program
A graphics program that allows users to draw on screen by icons such as brush, eraser, lasso, pencil, scissors, spray paint, with a mouse or other pointing device. Popular ones include PC Paintbrush (for IBM PCs and compatibles) and MacPaint (for Macintosh computers).

palette
The complete range of color choices.

palmtop
Tiny computer that literally fits in the palm of your hand.

Pantone Matching System
A professional color matching system.

paper feed
The movement of paper through a printer.

paper white display
An easy-on-the-eyes high end monitor featuring the stark contrast of black characters on a white screen.

Paradox
A database program for IBM PCs and compatibles.

parallel interface
An electronic path for the simultaneous flow of two or more bits of data.

parallel port
The port that supports parallel processing to peripheral devices, such as printers.

parallel printer
A printer that connects to a parallel port.

parallel processing
See *multitasking*.

parameters
Defining characteristics.

parameter RAM (PRAM)
The portion of RAM in a Macintosh computer that stores configuration information.

parent directory
The directory above the directory currently in use.

parity
The characteristic of being odd or even.

parity bit
An extra bit added to data for parity checking.

parity checking
Checks that data has been precisely transmitted or copied by adding up the number of bits and comparing it to the number of bits in the original data.

parity error
An error caught in a parity check.

park
Positioning a hard disk's read/write head drive in a safe position so that it will not be damaged when the drive is moved.

parse
Separating transferred data into separate columns to fit correctly in a spreadsheet.

partition
A section of memory on a hard disk that is isolated so that it is treated as a separate disk by the operating system.

Pascal
A high level programming language that requires a very structured, methodical design of programs.

password
A security identification tool that limits access to multi-user systems.

paste
After "cutting," replacing a section of type in a document.

path
The route a program follows to access information.

PATH
A DOS and OS/2 command that instructs the operating system which directories to search.

path name
The name that identifies a file and the path DOS and OS/2 systems must take to find a file.

pause
Temporarily stop.

PC (Personal Computer)
A relatively small, self-contained computer designed for individual users, that contains all the hardware and software needed to perform tasks.

PCB (Printed Circuit Board)
A thin rectangular plate of electronic components such as chips that are used to run a computer.

PCL (Printer Control Language)
The page description language recognized by Hewlett Packard LaserJet and compatible printers.

PC Paintbrush
A paint program for IBM PCs and compatibles.

PC Tools
A package of file and disk management utility programs for Macintosh and IBM PCs and compatibles.

PCX
A standard file format that stores object-oriented graphics in device-independent form, enabling them to work in different systems and programs.

PDL
See page description language.

peer-to-peer architecture
A local area network with no file server, where each workstation has equal capabilities and access to the public files of all the other workstations.

pel
Short for pixel.

peripheral
External devices that are connected to and controlled by a computer, such as a printer, monitor, keyboard, modem or mouse.

personal computer
See PC.

personal information manager (PIM)
Programs that help users organize personal information, with features such as notebooks, address books,
appointment calendars.

phono plug
A short-stemmed connector that connects audio
devices to the computer.

physical
Pertaining to hardware, as opposed to logical or
virtual, which refer to software.

physical format
See low level format.

pica
A typography measurement equal to approximately
1/6 inch or 12 points.

PICT file format
An object oriented graphics file format for Macintosh
computers.

PIM
See personal information manager.

pin feed
See tractor feed.

pins
The points that press on an ink ribbon to make dots
on a dot-matrix printer. The more pins, the higher
quality the image produced.

pipe
A temporary software connection that redirects the
output of one command so that it becomes the input
of another.

pitch
In typography, a unit of measure equal to the number
of characters printed per inch.

pixel (PIcture ELement)
The smallest single point in a graphics image.

planar board
The motherboard of an IBM PS/2 computer.

pla

plasma display

A type of flat panel display commonly used in laptop computer screens that works by energizing ionized gas trapped between two transparent panels. Same as gas plasma display.

platform

The basic hardware or software standard on which a computer system is based. Same as hardware platform.

platform independence

The ability of a local area network to link computers with different platforms, such as Macintosh and IBM PCs and compatibles.

platter

The round magnetic part(s) of a hard disk.

plot

Creating an image by drawing lines.

plotter

A printer that creates images by moving ink pens over the surface of the paper. Commonly used for computer aided design.

plug

Hardware that connects two devices.

plug compatible

The ability to connect to devices of different manufacturers without alterations.

point

In typography, a unit of measure equal to 1/72 of an inch.

pointer

An on-screen arrow or other symbol indicating the position of the mouse.

pointing device

An input device that controls the movement of the on-screen pointer, such as a mouse.

polling

The continuous requesting of data from one device to another.

pop up utility
A memory resident program that can be executed from other programs by pressing a hot key. *See **TSR program***.

pop up menu/window
A menu/window that appears on-screen when a hot key is pressed.

popping
In programming, removing data from a stack. The opposite of pushing.

port
A plug on a computer to which peripheral devices are connected.

portable
Small. Lightweight. Designed to be easily transported.

portrait
In word processing, printing a page vertically, across the shorter length of paper.

post
To record data.

PostScript
A simple interpretive programming language with powerful graphics capabilities, used primarily for printing documents on laser printers.

posture
In typography, the slant of characters.

power down
Turn off.

power line filter
A device that plugs into your power source and your computer to smooth out voltage fluctuations that could damage a computer.

power supply
Whatever supplies power to your computer, usually a standard electrical outlet.

power up
Turn on.

power user
An expert computer user.

PowerPoint
A presentation graphics software program.

ppm (Pages Per Minute)
A measure of the speed of printers.

PRAM
See parameter RAM.

precision
In floating point numbers, refers to the number of digits past the decimal.

presentation graphics
Professional images for business presentations and reports, i.e., charts, graphs, etc.

Presentation Manager
A windows-based program designed by Microsoft for the IBM OS/2 System.

preview
In word processing, displaying a formatted document on the screen to see exactly what the printed page will look like. Same as page preview.

primary storage
The computer's main memory.

print engine
The mechanism inside a laser printer that creates an image and transfers it to paper.

print server
The device that controlls access to a printer in a local area network.

print spooling.
See spooling.

printed circuit board
See PCB.

printer
Device that uses various means to transfer images to paper.

printer driver
A file that contains the information your computer needs to work with a particular type/brand of printer.

printer font
A font that can be printed, not just displayed on-screen. There are 3 types: built-in fonts, cartridge fonts and downloadable fonts.

printout
See hard copy.

PRN
The default printer port in DOS and OS/2 systems.

procedure
How a specific task is performed.

processing
When the CPU executes program instructions and sorts or changes data in some other manner.

processor
Short for microprocessor or CPU.

PROCOMM PLUS
A popular telecommunications program for IBM PCs and compatibles.

Prodigy
A popular on-line service that offers home shopping, news, stock quotes, bulletin boards, an encyclopedia and more.

program
An organized list of instructions that tell the computer exactly what to do.

programmable read-only memory
See PROM.

program generator
A program that prompts users to perform certain steps to issue commands, such as setting parameters for a database search.

program overlay
Part of a program stored on a disk for use only when necessary.

programmer
A person who can write computer programs.

programmer's switch
A switch that enables Macintosh users to reset and debug the computer without turning the power on and off.

programming languages
Languages, each with its own patterns and key words, used to program computers. High level languages include BASIC, C, COBOL, FORTRAN and Pascal.

project management program
Programs that keep track of all the separate parts of a project.

PROM (Programmable Read-Only Memory)
A computer chip that, once programmed, can never be changed.

PROMPT
An internal command for DOS and OS/2 systems that customizes the prompt.

prompt
An on-screen word or symbol that tells you that the computer is waiting for you to do something, such as enter a password or other information.

proportional pitch
See proportional spacing.

proportional spacing (PS)
A font where the space allotted to each character varies according to the width of the character. Same as proportional pitch.

proprietary
Private, not for public use. A technology or device to be used solely by the owner, not by a competitor.

protected mode
A mode for utilizing memory (for later model Intel microprocessors on IBM PCs and compatibles) that prevents system failures during multitasking operations.

protocol
See **communications protocol**.

PrtSc key
A key on IBM PC and compatible keyboards that tells the printer to print whatever image is on the screen.

PS/2
See **IBM Personal System/2**.

public domain software
See freeware.

pull-down menu
A menu with a vertical list of command options that appear when selected by a mouse or enter key.

pushing
In programming, to add data to a stack. The opposite of popping.

Q & A
A combination word processing and database program for IBM PCs and compatibles.

QBE
See **Query By Example**.

QIC (Quarter Inch Cartridge)
Full size or mini cartridge tape used as a back up storage medium for personal computers.

QuarkXPress
A page layout program that incorporates some word processing features.

Quattro Pro
A popular spreadsheet program.

query
A question that requests specific information from a database.

qui

query by example (QBE)
A method of requesting information from a database with the help of prompts that request specific search criteria.

query language
An database information retrieval language.

queue
A series of jobs for the computer to execute one after another.

QuickBasic
A high level programming language popular for windows-based programs.

QuickDraw
The basic graphics display system for Macintosh computers.

Quicken
An accounting/checkbook management program for IBM PCs and compatibles and Macintosh computers.

QWERTY keyboard
The layout of keys on a standard typewriter style keyboard; the first six letters on the top alphabetic line.

radio buttons
A group of graphical user interface buttons that appear in a dialog box. Selecting one automatically deselects the others.

radio frequency interference (RFI)
Disrupting electrical interference on the radio frequency spectrum.

ragged
In word processing, not aligned along a margin. Opposite of justified.

RAM (Random Access Memory)
The computer's main memory, where program instructions and data are stored so that they can be accessed randomly — without affecting other data. The most common type of memory found in computers.

RAM cache
Same as cache memory.

RAM disk
Random access memory that has been reconfigured to act like a disk drive. Same as virtual disk.

RAMDRIVE.SYS
The DOS systems configuration file that reconfigures part of the random access memory to act like a disk drive.

RAM resident
Permanently in memory. Same as memory resident.

random access
The ability to directly access random bits of memory, without going through a predefined sequence of locations.

random access memory
See RAM.

range
In spreadsheet programs, a cell or group of adjoining cells.

range format
The numeric format choice that applies to a specific range of cells in a spreadsheet program worksheet.

range name
A name given to a specific range of cells in a spreadsheet program worksheet.

raster graphics
Same as bit-mapped graphics.

raster image processor (RIP)
The device in a laser printer that transfers the image to the drum of the print engine line by line.

raw data
Data that has not been arranged or edited.

read

To copy data from a disk or other storage medium into the computer's main memory, where it can be accessed by a program.

readme file

Program information, usually not included with hard copy documentation, often containing recent updates and installation instructions.

read only

The ability to view but not modify or delete data on a storage medium.

read only memory

See ROM.

read/write

The ability to view and modify or delete data on a storage medium.

real address

Same as absolute address.

real mode

When Intel microprocessors are given a specific storage location and direct access to peripheral devices.

real time

Right now; immediately responsive.

real time clock

Battery powered computer clocks that keep time even when the machine is turned off.

reboot

Restart.

recalculate

Calculations that encompass the values of spreadsheet cells.

record

Complete information.

record-oriented

A database management program that displays records in response to queries, as opposed to tables.

recover

To restore the computer to a previous state.

RECOVER

A DOS and OS/2 command to retrieve salvageable data from a file with bad sectors.

recto

The right-hand page in two sided printing.

redirection

The rerouting of input/output functions to someplace other than the default I/O device.

redlining

In word processing, marking a section of text with an attribute (such as double underline or distinctive color) to indicate that it has been edited.

reduced instruction set computer (RISC)

A CPU where processing capabilities have been reduced to increase speed.

reformat

In word processing, to change the design of a page. In computer systems, changing the formatting of a secondary storage disk.

refresh

To invigorate or rejuvenate. Dynamic RAM must be continually refreshed or it will lose stored data.

register

An area in a CPU where data is stored before it is processed.

Relational DataBase Management System (RDBMS)

A relational database management program to create, install and maintain customized database applications.

relational operator

A symbol such as = (equal to), > (greater than), < (less than), that indicates the relationship between two values.

relative address
An address specified according to its distance from another location, as opposed to absolute address, which is a fixed location in the memory of the CPU.

release number
Specifies an updated version of a program.

remote
Refers to hardware at a distant location, not directly connected to your computer.

removable storage
Any secondary storage medium designed as a self-enclosed cartridge that can be easily removed from the computer.

repagination
In word processing, renumbering pages in a document.

repeat key
A key that, when held down, enters the same character over and over again until it is released.

repeater
A device used to extend the reach of cables in a local area network.

replace
In some word processing programs, a function that searches for a specific word or phrase and replaces it with another. Same as search and replace.

reserved words
Key words, designated with special meanings by the program, that cannot be used for any other purpose.

reset button
A button that restarts the computer without turning power off and on.

resident
Permanently in memory. Same as memory resident, RAM resident.

resident font
Same as internal font.

resolution
The sharpness of an image.

restore
In a windows environment, to return a window to it's original size.

return
See hard return, soft return, enter/RETURN key.

reverse video
Highlighting of normally dark characters as light on a dark background and of normally light characters as dark on a light background.

RGB monitor (Red, Green, Blue)
A monitor that accepts separate red, green and blue signals to display color images.

RightWriter
A program that checks grammar and punctuation.

ring network
A ring-shaped local area network design where nodes are connected to and can share data with each other.

RISC
See reduced instruction set computer.

ripple through effect
When ERROR messages suddenly appear throughout a spreadsheet program as a result of a change in the formula that has corrupted existing data.

river
In a page layout, when the eye is drawn to a flowing pattern of white space.

RLL (Run Length Limited)
A method of storing and retrieving data on a hard disk that increases access speed and the amount of data that can be stored by as much as 50%.

RMDIR
A DOS and OS/2 command to delete an empty subdirectory from a disk.

ROM (Read Only Memory)
The part of a computer's memory that contains prerecorded data and does not lose its contents when power fails or is turned off. Contains essential system programs that can only be read, they cannot be erased.

ROM BIOS
See BIOS.

root directory
The top level directory, formed on DOS systems when the disk is formatted. In DOS systems, the symbol for the root directory is \.

root name
In DOS systems, the beginning one to eight characters of a DOS file name.

routine
The part of a program that executes a particular task.

row
A horizontal line of cells in a spreadsheet.

row-wise recalculation
Recalculating cells in a spreadsheet row by row, one right after another.

RS-232
A standard sanctioned by the Electronic Industries Association for sending asynchronous data communications.

RS-232C
A standard sanctioned by the Electronic Industries Association for connecting serial devices such as modems to IBM PCs and compatibles.

RS-422/423
A standard sanctioned by the Electronic Industries Association for connecting serial devices such as modems to Macintosh computers.

rule
On a page layout, a thin straight line. In programming, a statement that governs the reactions of the system to a given situation.

ruler
An on-screen device for measuring sections of a page layout, and setting margins and tabs.

run
To execute a program.

run length limited
See RLL.

run time error

An error that occurs while a program is running, as opposed to a compile time error that occurs while a program is being compiled.

run time version

A version of a program that includes another, limited use application. For example, many programs come with a run time version of Windows, which loads each time the program is used (but cannot be used with any other program), allowing users without Windows to use some Windows-based programs.

SAA

See Systems Application Architecture.

sans serif

A typeface without serifs.

save

In word processing, to copy a file to a storage medium.

sawtooth distortions

See aliasing.

scalable font

A typeface that can be produced in any size or scale.

scale

Resizing an object or font without changing its configuration.

scanner

See optical scanner.

scissoring

A means of trimming a computerized image to size by selecting a frame size, placing the frame over the graphic, then cropping the graphic to fit the frame.

scrapbook

A Macintosh desk accessory that stores frequently used graphics.

screen capture
Storing whatever is on the screen.

screen dump
Printing whatever is on the screen. Same as snapshot.

screen saver
A program that helps prolong a monitor's life by saving it from permanent ghosting. It works by blacking out the screen and/or displaying a moving pattern when it is untouched for more than a few minutes. As soon as a key is depressed, the original display reappears.

screen font
An on-screen representation of a bit-mapped printed font.

script
A list of commands for the computer to perform.

scroll
To view more of a document by moving the on-screen display up or down, left or right.

scroll bar/box
A bar that appears along the side and/or bottom of the display screen that allows users to select and move to areas of a document by clicking on the scroll bar with the mouse.

Scroll Lock key
A key on IBM PC and compatible keyboards that, in some programs, switches the arrow keys from one mode to another.

SCSI (Small Computer Systems Interface)
Pronounced "scuzzy." An interface standard for attaching peripheral devices to computers.

search and replace
See replace.

secondary storage
A storage medium such as a disk or tape that stores data even when power is off.

sector
A segment of one of the concentric circles that make up a formatted disk.

security
Protecting computers and stored data from unauthorized users.

seek time
The time it takes for a program to retrieve data.

select
To choose an icon or section of text by clicking on the mouse or, if your choice is highlighted, hitting enter.

semiconductor
A material, like silicon, that is neither a good conductor of electricity nor a good insulator. Computer chips are made of semiconductor materials.

sequence control structure
Instructs the computer to execute program statements in the order in which they are written.

sequential access
Reading and/or writing data by moving through a sequence of stored data items.

serial communications
When data is transmitted one bit at a time, as opposed to parallel communications, in which several bits are transmitted at the same time.

serial interface
See serial port.

serial mouse
A mouse that connect to a computer's serial port.

serial port
A port for serial communication, that also makes sure that transmissions and receptions occur without loss of data. Same as serial interface.

serif
The small decorative line used to embellish the main stroke of a letter.

server
The computer or device that provides services for computers in a network.

shadowing

A process to increase the computer's speed by setting aside a portion of RAM and using it instead of the slower ROM for some basic functions like booting up.

shareware

Software that's free on a trial basis; if you like it, and want to use it, you are expected to pay a small fee for it.

sheet feeder

The device that feeds single sheets of paper into a printer. Same as cut sheet feeder.

shell

The outer layer of a program, the one that users interface with to run the program. Designed to make complicated programs more user friendly.

shift click

The act of holding down the shift key and clicking the mouse at the same time. Used in Windows and Macintosh systems to select more than one item.

shift key

A toggle key to use uppercase letters. On some keyboards, labeled "CAPS LOCK."

shut down

Turn off.

SideKick

A popular utility program for Macintosh and IBM PCs and compatibles that provides an address book, appointment calendar, notepad, calculator and more.

SIG

See special interest group.

sign

A symbol (+ or -) to indicate whether a number has a positive or negative value.

signal

An electrical event that conveys information.

silicon chip

See chip.

SIMM (Single In-line Memory Module)
A small, easily installed circuit board that adds 256K or
1M of RAM to a computer.

simulation
A fabricated model that enables the computerized
exploration of specific properties, i.e., simulating a
new wing design on an airplane to test its feasibility.
Widely used in aeronautical engineering, education,
computer games, etc.

single density disk
A floppy disk, with only one side prepared for storing
data, now nearly obsolete. Most disks are now double
density.

site license
When a software publisher allows an organization to
make copies of a program for internal use at a cost
that's less than buying that number of programs.
Same as software license.

size
To make something larger or smaller.

skip factor
Instructing a program to skip a number of data points
when designing a chart or graph, so that the layout is
less cluttered.

slate PC
A personal computer that accepts input from an
electronic pen instead of a keyboard.

slot
See expansion slot.

slug
The code in headers and footers to signal the insertion
of a page number.

Small Computer System Interface
See SCSI.

smart terminal
A terminal with some processing capabilities: more
than a dumb terminal, less than an intelligent terminal.

smoothing
A technique used by some laser printers to make curved lines appear smoother.

snaking columns
See newspaper columns.

snapshot
Printing whatever is on the screen. Same as screen dump.

SNOBOL
A high level programming language for text processing applications.

soft
In computers, refers to something intangible, easily changed or not permanent, i.e., software, soft return.

soft cell boundary
In a spreadsheet program, the ability to enter more characters than the cell usually allows.

soft font
A font loaded into a printer's memory that can be easily erased.

soft hyphen
See hyphenation.

soft page break
A page break inserted by a word processing program to ensure that current text falls within set margins. Automatically changes as text is added or deleted.

soft return
A line break inserted by a word processing program to ensure that line length falls with set margins. Automatically changes as text is added or deleted.

soft-sectored disk
An unformatted disk.

soft start
See warm boot.

software
Computer-readable and storable data or instructions.

software engineering
The science of improving the production of computer software.

software license
See site license.

software package
All the components for an application program, including support and utility programs and documentation.

software piracy
The unauthorized duplication of copyrighted software.

software protection
See copy protection.

sort
Reorder data.

sort key
The field in a database management program that determines the way data is arranged. For example, by last name, by city, etc.

source code
Programming instructions as they are actually written, before they're translated into machine language.

source file
The file that program instructions are copied from.

Special Interest Group (SIG)
Computer users who get together — electronically or personally — to discuss matters of common interest. Same as users group.

speech recognition
See voice recognition.

speech synthesis
Computer-generated sounds that resemble human speech. Same as voice synthesis.

spell checker
A word processing mode that checks the spelling of words in a document.

split screen
Dividing a display screen into two windows that can display two different documents.

spooling (Simultaneous Peripheral Operations On-Line)
Routing jobs to be printed to a buffer, which releases them when the printer is ready to print, allowing users to continue to work on the computer while printing takes place. Same as print spooling.

spreadsheet
A table of values arranged in rows and columns, similar to an accountant's worksheet. Same as worksheet.

spreadsheet program
Programs that allow users to electronically manipulate and calculate rows and columns of data.

SQL
See Structured Query Language.

SRAM (Static Random Access Memory)
Pronounced ess-ram. A RAM memory chip that is faster, more dependable and needs to be refreshed less often than DRAM.

ST-412 interface
Same as ST-506 interface.

ST-506 interface
The standard interface for connecting hard disk drives to IBM PCs and compatibles.

stack
A data structure that removes items in a Last In, First Out (LIFO) order.

stack overflow
Error message that occurs when the LIFO order isn't followed.

stand-alone
Self-contained.

standard
A set of criteria for performance that is accepted as the industry norm.

star network
A local area network with a star configuration.

start bit
In asynchronous communications, a signal that precedes the transmission of a byte of data.

statement
A computer command written in a high-level programming language.

static RAM
See SRAM.

static variable
An unchanging variable.

stem
A letter's principal vertical line.

stop bit
In asynchronous communications, a signal that follows the transmission of a byte of data.

storage
The retention of data.

storage device
Any medium for storing data.

store
To copy data.

string
See character string.

strikeout
On some word processors, an attribute used to mark deleted text by overtyping with a slash or other symbol.

string
Series.

Structured Query Language (SQL)(Pronounced sequel)
A popular query language for requesting information from a database.

style sheet
A format for the layout of a document.

stylus
A pen-like device used directly on the screen for drawing or selecting menu options.

subdirectory
A directory within a directory. *See **directory***.

submenu
A menu within a menu. *See **menu***.

subroutine
See routine.

subscript
In word processing, a character that prints slightly below the typing line.

suitcase
In Macintosh systems, an icon indicating a font or accessory not yet installed in the System Folder.

supercomputer
Very expensive computer (upwards of $1 million) that executes a few programs very fast. Used for specialized applications that require enormous amounts of mathematical calculations.

SuperPaint
An illustration program for Macintosh systems that combines the bit-mapped graphics of MacPaint with the object-oriented graphics of MacDraw.

superscript
A character that prints slightly above the typing line.

super VGA
See SVGA.

support
The ability to do something. For example, a word processor that supports graphics is one that has graphics capabilities; a printer that supports a certain font is capable of printing that font.

surge
A brief, unexpected burst of increased electric voltage.

surge protector
A device that offers protection from power surges, which can damage a computer.

SVGA (Super VGA)
Offers sharper resolution than VGA. Same as VGA Plus.

swap
Replace or exchange.

synchronous communication
Very high speed data communication synchronized by recurring electronic signals.

syntax
The spelling, grammar and other rules that govern a programming language.

syntax error
When the precise rules of a programming language are not followed, an error occurs.

sysop (SYStem OPerator)
The person in charge of a bulletin board on a public network.

System
Along with Finder, makes up the desktop and file management system for Macintosh computers.

system board
See motherboard.

system date
The date stored and maintained in a computer's memory.

system disk
A disk containing the computer's operating system and all files needed to start the computer.

system file
A file containing information used by the operating system, as opposed to files with information used by programs.

system folder
A folder that contains the file management system for Macintosh computers.

system prompt
An on-screen prompt indicating that the operating system is available for routine tasks such as copying files, formatting disks and loading programs.

systems analyst
A person who designs, manages and/or implements a business system.

systems software
All the software — including operating system and utility programs — needed to operate and maintain a computer system.

system unit
See *CPU*.

tab key
A key that moves the cursor a preset number of blank spaces.
Also often used to move the cursor through on-screen menus.

table
Data presented in rows and columns.

table utility
A word processing format that creates a template of rows and columns for text.

Tagged Image File Format (TIFF)
A high resolution bit mapped graphics format for storing scanned images on IBM PCs and compatibles and Macintosh computers.

tape
A secondary data storage medium.

tape backup unit
A device to copy hard disk data onto magnetic tape at high speeds.

tape drive
A device that reads and stores data onto magnetic tape, much like a standard tape recorder.

target
Destination.

task
A procedure or job performed by the computer.

technical support
Personalized, professional problem-solving advice.

telecommunications
Transmitting information over telephone lines.

telecopy
A fax transmission.

Telenet
A large public data network that provides log-on services to many commercial on-line computer services.

teletype (TTY) display mode
Displaying characters on a monitor line by line, as they are received. DOS systems use TTY display mode.

template
In word processing, a diagram or listing of key functions for a particular program than can be mounted on the keyboard for easier identification. Also, any document or worksheet containing frequently used text or graphics, such as a letterhead.

terabyte
A unit of memory equal to approximately 1 trillion bytes.

terminal
In multiuser systems, an input/output device such as a keyboard and display monitor, but no CPU.

terminal emulation
The process of making a computer react like a terminal, often to gain access to a mainframe or bulletin board.

terminate and stay resident program
See *TSR program*.

tex

text editor
A program that makes writing and editing computer programs easier.

text file
A file consisting solely of ASCII characters, containing no other codes or control characters.

text mode
Setting a video adapter to display only ASCII codes, as opposed to video mode, which can display bit-mapped images. Same as character mode.

text wrap
When words literally wrap around a graphic element.

TFT (Thin Film Transistor)
An expensive, very high resolution flat panel display screen.

thermal printer
The kind of printer found in most FAX machines and calculators that produces low-quality images by pressing heated pinheads against heat-sensitive paper.

thin film transistor
See **TFT**.

three-dimensional spreadsheet
A spreadsheet program that allows users to create and use more than one spreadsheet at a time by stacking the pages.

throughput
The time it takes a computer to send data through all components of the system and process information, typically measured in bits per second.

thumbnail
A miniature representation of text or graphics.

TIFF
See **Tagged Image File Format**.

timed backup
A function that automatically saves work at predetermined intervals.

time sharing
When multiple users literally share a network's computer resources.

title bar

An on-screen bar with the name of the file, usually located on top of a window.

toggle switch

A key that switches back and forth from one setting to another.

token

A single element of a programming language. Also, a special series of bits in a token ring network.

token ring network

A local area network in a circle configuration. Messages are sent when one computer attaches a message to a special bit pattern (called a token) as it travels around the circle.

toner

Special kind of ink used in laser printers and copy machines.

topology

See network topology.

TOPS

A local area network program that links IBM PCs and compatibles and Macintosh computers in one distributed processing system.

touch screen

A touch-sensitive display screen, where users can interact with the computer and select options by simply pointing with a finger instead of using a pointing device such as a mouse.

tower configuration

When a computer's power supply, motherboard and mass storage devices are arranged one on top of the other.

TPI (Tracks Per Inch)

A measurement of the density of tracks on a disk.

track

One of many rings on a floppy or hard disk where data can be encoded.

trackball

An input device that moves the pointer on the screen when the user rotates a ball, instead of moving the entire device (like a mouse).

tracks per inch

See TPI.

tractor feed

A sprocket-wheel mechanism for feeding fan-fold paper into and out of a printer. Same as pin feed.

traffic

A measurement of the volume of transmissions sent over a communications network.

transaction processing

A system where a computer responds instantly to individual user requests, like an ATM (Automatic Teller Machine). The opposite of batch processing.

transactional application

A program that creates and maintains one shared database on a local area network.

transfer rate

Measures the number of bits of data transferred per second from a disk to the CPU.

translate

To convert a program or data from one format to another.

transparent

An action that takes place without user notice.

transportable

Lightweight, portable.

transpose

To switch the order of characters, words or sentences.

tree structure

A way of organizing information with each element attaching to one or more elements directly beneath it, like the trunk and branches of a tree.

Trojan Horse

A benign-looking program that contains hidden, destructive codes that can severely damage, even wipe out data on the hard disk.

truncate
To abbreviate or cut off, as in rounding off very long decimal numbers.

TSR (Terminate and Stay Resident) program
A program that, once loaded, remains in RAM and can be activated any time, even while other programs are running. Common TSRs include spell checkers, calculators, thesauruses and notepads.

TTL (Transistor Transistor Logic)
A special kind of digital circuit, or any type of digital input or device.

turnkey system
Complete set up of all hardware and software needed to run a particular application.

Tymnet
A large public data network that provides log-on services to many commercial on-line computer services.

tutorial
Step-by-step, guided instructions.

twisted pair cable
A low bandwidth connecting cable.

type
Entering characters by depressing keys on a keyboard.

TYPE
An internal DOS and OS/2 command to display a file on-screen.

typeface
Characters and numbers in a common, distinctive design.

typeover
See overstrike/overtype.

typesetting
Producing high quality type for reproduction.

undelete
To restore all or part of a file or document that has been deleted.

underflow error
What happens when a computer tries to represent a number that is smaller than its predefined range of values.

undo
Returning to a previous condition by retracting the most recent command. Some programs support an unlimited number of undos. Some have a special undo key.

uninterruptable power supply (UPS)
A back-up battery charged by line current that turns on when the main power supply fails.

Universal Asynchronous Receiver/Transmitter (UART)
An integrated circuit that transforms a computer's parallel data stream to the serial data stream needed for asynchronous communications.

UNIX
A popular multiuser multitasking operating system.

unpack
To restore a compressed file back to its original form.

upgrade
To move up to a later version of a software program or a newer or more powerful piece of hardware.

upload
To transmit data from your computer to another.

uppercase
Capital letters.

UPS
See *uninterruptable power supply*.

upward compatibility
Software that can run on newer and/or more powerful versions of the computer it was designed to run on.

USENET
A large wide area network that serves as a bulletin board for many UNIX computer systems.

user
One who operates a computer.

user-defined
Chosen by the user.

user-friendly
Easy (or easier) to use.

users group
See special interest group.

user interface
The commands or menus used by a user to communicate with a program.

user memory
See conventional memory.

utility program
A program that performs tasks to help users manage system resources and improve efficiency.

UUCP
The international wide area network that links UNIX computers.

vaccine
A program to detect the presence of a computer virus.

value
The numeric quantity of a data element.

value added reseller (VAR)
A company that improves upon hardware manufactured by another company.

vaporware
A mocking term for software that is heavily promoted but not yet available.

VAR
See value added reseller.

variable
A symbol or sign representing a value that may change during a program's execution.

VDT (Video Display Terminal)
Monitor, display screen. Same as VDU.

VDT radiation
The radiation emitted by VDTs.

VDU (Video Display Unit)
See VDT.

vector graphics
See object oriented graphics.

vendor
One who sells computers, peripherals and/or software.

Ventura Publisher
A page layout program for IBM PCs and compatibles.

VER
In DOS and OS/2 systems, an internal command to display the current DOS version number.

VERIFY
In DOS and OS/2 systems, an internal command to verify that data on a disk is properly stored.

verso
The left-hand page in two sided printing.

vertical justification
Aligning vertical columns on a page, adding space (leading) between lines where necessary, to ensure that all columns align evenly at the bottom of the page.

vertical scroll
To view more of a document by moving the on-screen display up or down.

very large scale integration (VLSI)
Placing a hundred thousand or more electronic components on a single chip.

VGA (Video Graphic Array)
A high resolution color graphics system for IBM PCs and compatibles that supports as many as 256 colors and provides higher resolution than CGA or EGA.

VGA Plus
See SVGA.

video adapter
An expansion board that provides enhanced display capabilities.

video display board
Same as video adapter.

video disk
An optical disk containing pictures and sound that are played back on a video disk player attached to a standard television monitor.

video monitor
See monitor.

video mode
Setting a video adapter to display bit-mapped images, as opposed to text mode, which can only display ASCII characters.

video RAM
See VRAM.

video standards
Standards that define the resolution and colors for video display monitors.

view
Displaying on-screen the information in a database that meets user-specified criteria.

virtual
Apparent or conceptual, as opposed to actual or real.

virtual disk
See RAM disk.

virtual machine
The on-screen simulation of a fabricated computer.

virtual memory
Extending the size of a computer's RAM by using part of the hard disk.

virus
A destructive, self-replicating computer program than can wreck havoc with systems.

VLSI
See very large scale integration.

voice mail
A communications system that stores voice messages.

voice recognition
The computer recognition of human speech. Same as speech recognition.

voice synthesis
See speech synthesis.

VOL
A DOS and OS/2 internal command to display the volume label of the disk currently in use.

volatile memory
The part of the computer's memory (such as RAM) that relies on electronic or battery power to retain stored information and can be destroyed by power failures.

volume
The fixed amount of space on a storage medium.

volume label
The name assigned by a user to a disk or tape.

VRAM (Video Random Access Memory)
Special memory used by video adapters that can be accessed by two different devices at the same time.

wait state
A period of time when nothing happens. Programmed into many computer systems to allow slower components, such as RAM, to catch up with faster CPUs.

WAN (Wide Area Network)
Computers linked together in a relatively wide geographic area that share or exchange information.

warm boot
Resetting the computer while power is on.

warm link
When a change made to one file also changes data in another.

what-if inquiry
Investigating the implications on a database by changing key variables.

what you see is what you get
See *WYSIWYG*.

white space
The portion of a printed page left blank.

wide area network
See *WAN*.

widow
The last line of a paragraph that appears as the first line of a new page.

wild card
Characters that represent one or more other characters. For example, in DOS and OS/2 systems, an asterisk is a wild card that stands for any combination of letters; a question mark stands for any single character.

Winchester drive
See *hard disk drive*.

window

An enclosed, on-screen display area. Many window application programs allow a display screen to contain several windows, each running a different program or displaying a different file. *See Microsoft Windows*.

Windows

Short for Microsoft Windows.

word

In programming, one unit of memory storage.

Word

Short for Microsoft Word.

WordPerfect

A popular, full-featured word processing program for a variety of computers.

word processing

The act of creating, formatting and editing documents on a display screen via a keyboard, and storing them on a computer or dedicated word processor.

WordStar

A word processing program for CP/M and IBM PC and compatible computers.

word wrap

A word processing feature that automatically routes text to the next line when a line exceeds predefined margins. *See soft return*.

work group

A group of people, often on a local area network working together on a specific project.

worksheet

See spreadsheet.

workstation

A computer connected to a local area network.

WORM (Write Once, Read Many)

Technology that allows an optical storage disk to be encoded with data once (the data is permanent and cannot be changed or erased), but read any number of times.

worm
A special kind of computer virus than can replicate itself but not attach itself to other programs.

write
Recording information on a storage device.

write once, read many
See WORM.

write protect
To alter a disk (usually by covering or moving the write-protect tab) so that the information on it cannot be erased or modified.

WYSIWYG
(What You See Is What You Get)
Pronounced wizzy-wig. Where what you see on the display screen looks like what you'll see when the page is printed.

x-axis
Usually refers to the horizontal axis on a graph.

XGA (eXtended Graphics Array)
A high resolution color graphics system for IBM PCs and compatibles that supports more colors (25,000+) and provides higher resolution than CGA, EGA or VGA.

XCMD
*See **external command***.

XCOPY
In DOS and OS/2 systems, an external command to copy files from one or more subdirectories onto one disk or directory. In this process, as opposed to a BACKUP command, the original file is deleted.

x-height
The height of the lowercase letter x (as well as other lowercase letters without ascenders or descenders) in a particular typeface.

XMODEM
A popular asynchronous communications protocol that allows the transfer of one file at a time.

XOR operator

A Boolean operator that returns a value of TRUE when its two operands have different values.

XyWrite

Pronounced zi-rite. A popular word processing program for IBM PCs and compatibles.

y-axis

Usually refers to the vertical axis on a graph.

YMODEM

A popular asynchronous communications protocol that allows batch transfer, i.e., the transfer of many files at the same time.

zap

Wipe out, delete.

Zapf Dingbats

A popular set of ornamental symbols including scissors, pointing fingers, arrows, flowers and stars.

z-axis

The third dimension (depth) of a three dimensional graph.

zero wait state computer

Refers to computers that don't have to wait for slower components to catch up with faster ones. *See wait state*.

ZMODEM

A popular asynchronous communications protocol that's faster and detects errors better than XMODEM.

zoom

In a graphical user interface program, to enlarge or reduce the size of a window.

zoom box

A feature of some graphical user interface programs usually located in the corner of a window, that, when selected, enlarges the window to fill the screen.

#   #   #

More Quick Reference Guides

	Cat. No.		Cat. No.
AppleWorks	H-17	PC & MS DOS	X-17
dBase III Plus	B-17	Professional Write	P-17
dBase IV	B-18	Quattro Pro 4	Q-18
DOS 5	J-17	QuickBASIC	Y-17
Excel	E-18	Quicken 6	QB-17
Excel 4	A-18	Unix	U-17
Harvard Graphics for Windows	HG-17	Windows 3	N-17
Lotus 1-2-3 Intro	L-17	Windows 3.1	N3-17
Lotus 1-2-3 (Ver 2.2)	L2-17	Word 5.5	C-28
Lotus 1-2-3 (Ver 2.3)	L-18	Word 5 Mac	T-17
Lotus 1-2-3 (Ver 2.4)	K-18	WordPerfect 5.1	W-5.1
Lotus 1-2-3 (Ver 3.1)	J-18	WordPerfect for Windows	Z-17
Microsoft Works	K-17	WordStar 6.0	R-17
Multimate Adv II & Ver 4	G-17	Word for Windows	WN-17
OS/2 2.0	OS-17		

At your local bookstore, or by mail.   **$8.95**

------------------ORDER FORM------------------

(DDC) *Publishing*

14 E. 38 St., NY, NY 10016

Quantity Discounts
(800) 528-3897
ask for Jane Bond

$8.95 ea.

QTY.	CAT. NO.	DESCRIPTION

( ) Check enclosed. Add $2 for postage and handling.

( ) Visa ( ) MasterCard 800 528-3897

No._____ Exp. _____

Name_____

Firm_____

Address_____

City, State, Zip_____